The Old Union Canal
Guthrie Hutton

The lifting bridge at Fountainbridge is seen here in the 1920s at street level, with the Palais de Dance, later the Coliseum in the background.

The sheds beside Lochrin Basin look past their best in this drawing from about 1910.

The publishers regret that they cannot supply
copies of any pictures featured in this book.

Printed by Blissetts, Roslin Road, Acton, W3 8DH

Acknowledgements

It's difficult to know where to begin with a subject that has been familiar to me for most of my adult life (and I am no spring chicken!). I guess I have to thank everyone who I have known over the years and who has helped to form the memories that I have tapped to fill these pages. I will always value the friendships formed in the heat of campaigning battles for canal restoration, and the mud and mayhem of Drambuie Marathons. More directly I have to thank City of Edinburgh Council – www.capitalcollections.org.uk for the use of the pictures on pages 1, 4, 6, 8 and 10. These come from the wonderful collection of photographs taken by Francis M. Chrystal, a remarkable record of the canal, without which the true value of what was lost in the 1920s would not be known.

Further Reading

Also by Guthrie Hutton for Stenlake Publishing:
The Union Canal, A Capital Asset, 1993.
Scotland's Millennium Canals, 2002.
Shale Oil, A History of the Industry in the Lothians, 2010.

The books listed below were used by the author during his research. None are available from Stenlake Publishing; please contact your local bookshop or reference library.

A Companion for Canal Passengers Betwixt Edinburgh and Glasgow, 1823, (reprinted by the Linlithgow Union Canal Society, 1981).
Allan, J. K., *Their is a Cannal*, 1977.
Haynes, Nick, *Scotland's Canals*, 2015.
Lindsay, Jean, *The Canals of Scotland*, 1968.
Massey, Alison, *The Edinburgh and Glasgow Union Canal*, 1983.
Pratt, Edwin A, *Scottish Canals and Waterways*, 1922.
Ransom, P. J. G., *Scotland's Inland Waterways*, 1999.

Introduction

There was irritation in Edinburgh. Over in the west, that little upstart city Glasgow was growing fast, fuelled, literally, by cheaper coal than was available in the capital. Worse, there was coal in Mid and East Lothian, but mine owners operated a cartel to keep prices high and unscrupulous carters took advantage of poor transport links to sell short measure. Better transport infrastructure had curtailed such malpractice in Glasgow. Completed in 1790, the Forth & Clyde Canal linked the city to the east and west coasts and by 1793 boats carrying Lanarkshire coal could sail into Glasgow along the Monkland Canal. The lesson was not lost on Edinburgh: a canal to the west would reach new coalfields and reduce reliance on the Lothians.

Proposals made in the 1790s to link Edinburgh with the Monklands failed to attract investors. War then distracted attention, but the canal idea was revived when the harsh winter of 1812 that devastated Napoleon's army retreating from Moscow, also froze Edinburgh. Hugh Baird, the Forth & Clyde Canal Company's engineer, was asked to carry out a survey. He chose a less challenging route than the earlier proposals, using level ground through West Lothian and Stirlingshire to connect with the Forth & Clyde at Falkirk. There was outrage, and Robert Stevenson prepared a rival scheme less dependent on the Forth & Clyde and with a flight of locks connecting Leith Docks to the main canal. It was a costly option and when the great Thomas Telford indicated approval of Baird's proposal, investors were drawn to it.

With funding in place and parliamentary approval secured, work on the Edinburgh & Glasgow Union Canal began in March 1818. It was to be over 30 miles long and include three great aqueducts, over 60 bridges and a tunnel cut out of solid rock, but work proceeded quickly with only the tunnel causing a delay. The canal was open for business by May 1822 when a barge carrying stone from Denny arrived in Edinburgh. Coal from the west could also now reach the capital, but in response the Lothian coal masters reduced their prices, the canal had done its job, but had to fight for its future.

The venture was never a commercial success and any hope of an upturn evaporated when the Edinburgh & Glasgow Railway opened in 1842. The railway company bought the ailing canal in 1849 and by act of parliament had to maintain it in working condition. Had that not happened it could have crumbled into decay, but it struggled on into the 20th century with little commercial activity and some pleasure boating. In 1922 the Edinburgh basins were filled in, the Falkirk locks were abandoned in the 1930s and the remaining canal was closed in 1965. Culverts were subsequently installed to improve existing roads or build new ones, and a long section was filled in to make way for development of the Wester Hailes housing scheme.

The abandoned channel quickly filled with weed, silt and rubbish, but in the 1970s campaigning enthusiasts began to raise awareness. Their activities gathered momentum until, in the late 1990s, the Millennium Link project was launched to reinstate both the Union and Forth & Clyde Canals.

Manse Road Basin, Linlithgow about 1905.

A large crowd of people gathered to watch company chairman, Robert Downie of Appin, dig some turf and throw it into the air to indicate the start of construction work. The ceremony took place on the site where the Edinburgh terminal basin, Port Hopetoun, would be formed at the top of what later became known as Lothian Road. The canal port became a feature of the city's townscape with a number of coal merchants' yards and a large warehouse that projected into the basin. This was the arrival and departure point for passenger boats that plied between Edinburgh and the west. They were initially very busy, especially when, soon after the canal's opening, King George IV visited Edinburgh, an occasion inspired by Sir Walter Scott whose Waverley Novels also provided the names of the first two canal company passenger carrying boats, *Flora MacIvor* and *Di Vernon*. A hundred years after those halcyon early days Port Hopetoun had fallen on hard times, and soon after this picture was taken about 1920, the demolition men moved in.

36

MANIFEST OF THE BOAT, NO. 105

John Leighton Master, sailed for GLASGOW. 30 apl 183 0

	Tons.	Cwt.	Qrs.
13 Bags meal	1	12	2
33 Pieces Iron	1	18	"
4 Bales Canvas	1	"	"
4 Whds & 2 half Whds ale	1	5	"
2 Casks Seed	"	13	"
74 Boxes fruit	1	"	"
4 Boxes Types	"	7	"
3 Bags Barley	"	8	"
12 Boxes & Bales Cotton	2	9	"
Sundries	1	10	"
Lock 16 — Six Empty Punchens	"	12	"
Lock 16 — Sundries	2	"	"
Kirkintulloch 4 E Punchens	"	10	"
589–105 at Linlithgow Paper	15	4	2

Pro London, Leith, Edinburgh & Glasgow Shipping Co.

Passengers may have been the cream of canal carrying, but cargo was the bread and butter. Although stone was the first load to be carried from one end of the canal to the other and coal barges quickly became a familiar sight, other commodities were carried too as this manifest from 1830 shows. Heading for Glasgow, boat No.105 was loaded with bags of meal, pieces of iron, bales of cotton and many other items including ale, fruit, barley, and canvas. Along the way she appears to have transhipped some paper at Linlithgow from another boat and, on the Forth & Clyde Canal picked up other items at Lock 16 and Kirkintilloch. Loaded and unloaded by hand as individual items or packed in bags, bales, barrels and boxes it amounted to a substantial load in a heavy barge that a single horse moved step by trudging step from one side of the country to the other.

Although boat No.105 carried a variety of items, the vast majority of cargoes shipped along the canal were of a single commodity: coal. It came from pits in West Lothian, the Falkirk area and as far afield as the Monklands in Lanarkshire, a trade that increased after the opening of the Monkland and Kirkintilloch Railway in 1826. One of the principal mine owners using the canal was the Duke of Hamilton who sent prodigious quantities of coal into Port Hopetoun from his pits on the Slamannan plateau. To cope with the volume, a new basin named Port Hamilton was created on a site adjacent to Port Hopetoun, but separated from it by Semple Street. It looked like a keyhole when viewed from above or on a map an elongated rectangle with a rounded end for boats to turn. It is seen here about 1920 looking toward Morrison Street.

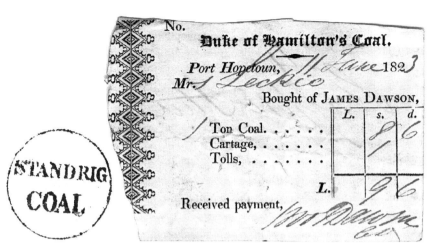

Duke of Hamilton's Coal.

No.

Port Hopetoun, 11 June 1823

Mr Leckie

Bought of JAMES DAWSON,

	L.	s.	d.
Ton Coal		8	6
Cartage, ...		1	
Tolls, ...			
L.		9	6

Received payment,

CALLENDER COAL.

SHIELHILL COAL

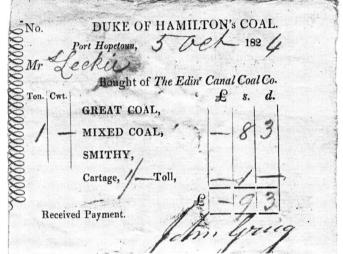

DUKE OF HAMILTON's COAL.

No.

Port Hopetoun, 5 Oct 1824

Mr Leckie

Bought of *The Edin' Canal Coal Co.*

Ton.	Cwt.		£	s.	d.
1	—	GREAT COAL,			
		MIXED COAL,	—	8	3
		SMITHY,			
		Cartage, 1/— Toll,	—	1	—
		£	—	9	3

Received Payment.

John Greig

STANDRIG COAL

No. 2. OLD BASIN, PORT HOPETOUN.

Mrs Leckie

Bought of Robert S. Dawson.

1831

Feby 24th

To 1 Ton Coal,	£ _ . 12 . _
.. Cartage,	
.. Tolls,	

Received payment,

Certified by

Wm Miller *Weigher*

Robt S. Dawson

John Alston

In this modern age when power comes at the flick of a switch, it is difficult to comprehend how important coal was to people in the early 19th century; they cared about their coal, where it came from and how it was handled. Not all coal was the same and discriminating customers could distinguish between the coals offered by individual collieries and came to know and trust favoured merchants. Large lumps, sometimes packed in straw and known as 'great coal', attracted a premium because buyers could see what they were getting. Smaller, broken lumps or mixtures of uncertain origin sold for less. This gave coal transported by barge an advantage, as it was less likely to be broken into small bits. A measure of the canal's coal trade can be gauged from these receipts; the 'Old Basin' refers to Port Hopetoun (Port Hamilton was known as the new basin) and the circular stamps indicate the source of the coal.

The advent of railways quickly spelled the end for passenger boats while the number of barges carrying coal, stone, bricks and other unglamorous commodities dwindled inexorably until, by the end of the 19th century the little-used terminal basins had sunk into seedy decline. They were seen as a blot on Edinburgh's classical image and just before the First World War the city authorities began the process of acquiring them. Delayed by the war, the canal ports were finally closed in 1922, the water drained and buildings demolished. A more enlightened age might have given the area a makeover and created a marina in the heart of the city, but instead a large tax office, Lothian House was built on the site of Port Hopetoun. The St. Cuthbert's Co-operative Association, whose headquarters building is on the left of this view looking toward Fountainbridge, was to have a similar impact on Port Hamilton.

The Edinburgh and Glasgow Railway, which had bought the canal in 1849 was itself taken over in 1865 by the North British Railway and it was they who sold the Port Hamilton site to the St. Cuthbert's Co-operative Association in 1921. St. Cuthbert's had begun trading from a small shop on Fountainbridge at the corner of Ponton Street in 1859 and had since then built up a considerable presence in the city with its headquarters adjacent to the canal at Fountainbridge. Like many co-operative societies it expanded to provide numerous goods and services and Port Hamilton was used for the development of a large bakery. Designed by the architect Thomas P. Marwick, the first part of the building was erected by the Association's own workforce and opened by the President, J. W. Thomson in March 1925. Its intended output was half-a-million two pound loaves in a six-day week.

When the city basins were drained in the 1920s, a new canal terminal was created to the west of Fountainbridge. Blunt-ended and hidden behind buildings it was called Lochrin Basin, a name that had originally been used for a small basin that branched off the main canal. It served Haig's distillery and after being abandoned by the early 20th century was used for a time as a skating pond. The new terminal was little used and it became isolated by the disused Leamington Bridge after the canal closed in 1965. The Forth Canoe Club moved in and rigged up slalom poles across the water, which would have irritated other boaters had there been any to be irritated. Boats did reappear after the canal's reopening and this unremarkable canal terminal underwent a renaissance when it was redeveloped as Edinburgh Quay, a complex of offices, hotels, and restaurants. One casualty of this makeover was the Port Hamilton Tavern, not the most sophisticated of pubs, but a much-lamented houff for drouthy drinkers.

The building on the facing page dominating the north side of Lochrin Basin was Castle Mills. Originally a silk mill, it was taken over in 1855 by Norris & Company, a firm started by Henry Lee Norris, a New Yorker who had been looking for a site in Scotland to set up a factory to make rubber boots, shoes, belting, packing and other goods. The company changed its name in 1857 to the North British Rubber Company and by the 1870s had started to make the solid rubber tyres needed by steam-driven traction engines. From these, the company graduated to make pneumatic tyres under the brand name 'Clincher'. A new tyre factory was erected alongside the eastern end of Lochrin Basin to meet demand after the First World War. The company also became noted for making golf balls. Following closure of the rubber works the site was redeveloped in the early 1970s for McEwan's Fountain Brewery, which is seen here reflected in the canal's mirror calm water. It remained in operation until 2005.

Designed and built by the Newcastle firm of Armstrong Whitworth, the splendid looking Leamington Bridge was originally erected in 1906 at Fountainbridge (see page 1). Unusually for an opening bridge the electrically-operated deck didn't tilt or swing, but was raised in a horizontal position to give a clearance of nine feet over the water level, while an up and over stepped footpath bridge allowed for uninterrupted pedestrian access. When erected it replaced a small opening bridge, one of four single-leaf bascule bridges that originally spanned the canal at Semple Street, Gilmore Park, Viewforth and Fountainbridge, but with the growth of road traffic this latter one was replaced. The lifting bridge was still relatively new when the city basins were closed in the 1920s so it was taken down and re-erected at Gilmore Park. It is seen here in the 1970s when the canal's decline and closure has caused the mechanism to become unusable, but since reopening it has been reinstated to give access to Edinburgh Quay.

While the canal was closed and Leamington Bridge was stuck shut, the large basin to the west of the bridge became the de facto Lochrin Basin. This was as far to the east as any boat could go, but as work to reinstate the canal was being done in 2004 it was discovered that this was also as far as at least one boat from an earlier time had gone. Before the improvement works started the basin was drained and there, on the offside, hidden in weed and covered by mud were the remains of an old sunk barge. Built of wood by craftsmen who knew and understood their trade and didn't need drawings, these simple, unglamorous craft were worked hard and discarded at the end of their life. None had survived. The discovery therefore represented a unique opportunity to find out how these boats were made and so, like a poor man's *Mary Rose* the remains were excavated and recorded by archaeologists – a rare sight in a canal basin.

The site where the archaeologists excavated the old barge was adjacent to Viewforth Bridge, which is seen in the distance in this 1970s view looking east, with the Fountain Brewery on the left and a clutter of workshop buildings and tenements on the right. The four original opening bridges were numbered separately to the stone bridges with Semple Street being Drawbridge No. 1, through to Drawbridge No. 4 at Viewforth. It was the first of these 'drawbridges' to be replaced, superseded by a substantial stone bridge with elaborately carved keystones representing the coat of arms of Edinburgh on the east side and on the west side Glasgow's coat of arms. No longer a drawbridge, it didn't fit with the numbering sequence of the stone bridges, although a slot on the keystones looks like a number one – all very confusing.

Going west from Viewforth Bridge the canal briefly takes on a character that, for a fertile imagination could conjure up images of dark Dickensian, melodrama set on gas-lit winter nights, dank swirling fog and footpads lurking in shadows beside the limpid water. Anyone who heard a cry, or a splash would be unable to help, thwarted by tall tenement buildings and high walls crowding in on each side, and bridges that span both canal and towpath with no access to or from the streets – like Luigi Pirandello's *Six Characters in Search of an Author* it's a location crying out for a dramatist. The cliff-like nature of the buildings has inspired an unofficial name, the 'city canyon', which is seen here at its western end in the 1970s. At this time the canal was closed, so someone evidently thought it appropriate to also shut off the towpath with a fence. It has since been removed, reinstating one of the canal's great assets.

The area to the west of the city canyon is more open as this view from the 1970s, looking east, shows. On the right is the imposing Polwarth Parish Church, also known as 'The Candlish' after Robert Smith Candlish, a prominent campaigner at the time of the Disruption of 1843, when the Free Church split from the Established Church of Scotland. The church was built 1899-1902, with the tower added a few years later. The city was expanding westward and in the late 19th century Harrison Park, on the left was created. It provided urban dwellers with open space and proved to be an ideal location for the Edinburgh Canal Society when it was formed in 1985. A couple of years later, the society also acquired a boathouse from a site further west along the canal and re-erected it in a slightly modified form in the lee of the Ashley Terrace Bridge. It was a colourful, attractive addition to both the canal and the park and gave the society a base for boating activities and an annual canal festival.

The city section of the canal had long been used for pleasure boating, a tradition continued by the Edinburgh Canal Society's collection of small boats, but one group of people took to the water, not just for fun but also for sport. Since 1846, when the St. Andrew Boat Club was established, rowing has been a constant presence on the canal, with Edinburgh University and some of the big city schools also erecting boathouses. The narrowness of the canal inevitably meant that boats could not race side by side, but inventive as ever the rowers devised a form of racing where one crew tried to row away from a boat behind them, which tried to catch the one in front. Despite the restrictions, the Union Canal has proved to be an ideal nursery for some of Britain's finest rowing talent like multiple Olympic medal winner Katherine Grainger, who was introduced to rowing on the canal during her student days. These rowers, photographed in 1995 are turning on the speed near Slateford Aqueduct.

Spanning the Water of Leith, the Slateford Aqueduct is one of three large aqueducts built to a standard construction; the others cross the Almond and Avon Rivers. Hugh Baird, who designed these magnificent structures, based his ideas on techniques developed by Thomas Telford, who also approved Baird's design. The key was to create a cast iron trough to contain the water and encase this with stone. A journalist who visited the aqueduct during construction likened the trough to a ship of enormous length: Slateford was 600 feet long and 65 feet high. Just to the east of this huge structure was another aqueduct carrying the canal across Slateford Road. Originally a single arched masonry structure, it was replaced in 1937 with a larger concrete arch, but the disruption caused by construction work halted the operation of brickworks barges from Winchburgh. This was the last commercial activity on the canal and it never resumed when the new aqueduct was completed and the canal reinstated.

Building materials accounted for a lot of canal traffic and if boatloads of bricks were a familiar sight toward the end of cargo carrying, stone was a major commodity in the early days. The stone came from a number of quarries alongside the canal with two of the biggest just to the west of Edinburgh at Hailes and Redhall. Less than half-a-mile apart, they both worked a bed of sandstone that differed in some characteristics from one quarry to the other. Redhall stone was regarded as superior and was used in the construction of many buildings in and around Port Hopetoun. The stone was shipped from the village of Stoneyport, seen here in a picture taken in December 1897. It's such an appropriate name, and has a certain charm, but it may predate the canal and refer, not to stone shipments but to an ancient stony path. Or maybe local folk, tongue in cheek, just adapted the old name to suit the new circumstances!

The great Glasgow-based Caledonian Railway opened its main line north from Carlisle to Carstairs in 1848. Branches from there to Glasgow and Edinburgh gave the 'Caley' a route between the cities, which, although longer and steeper than the more direct Edinburgh & Glasgow Railway led to fierce rivalry. This intensified after 1865 when the Edinburgh-based North British Railway (which had bought the canal in 1849) took over the Edinburgh & Glasgow. The Caledonian responded in July 1869 by opening a more direct route to Glasgow through the Calders, while maintaining its older line by way of Carstairs. The tracks spanned the Union Canal at Kingsknowe on the bridge seen here being crossed by a Caledonian passenger train. The picture is undated, but must have been taken before 1923 when the 'Caley' became part of the London Midland and Scottish Railway. The bridge in the picture has since been replaced by a more modern structure and the line electrified.

A field to the left of the bridge on the facing page shows that at the time the picture was taken, Kingsknowe was in the countryside, although the nearby Hailes Quarry was a major industrial presence. Beyond that, as this undated picture of Sighthill Bridge, No. 7, shows, the canal was in a rural setting, but that changed dramatically following closure in 1965. A drowned culvert was installed to replace the bridge at Kingsknowe Road. It was neither pretty nor user friendly, with steep steps on either side, which towpath users could climb up and over to cross the road, unless they were disabled in which case they were stuck. It was a reflection of negative attitudes toward canals, as if people in authority wished they weren't there, and in 1967 over a mile of the Union Canal was wished away when plans were put in place to build a giant new housing scheme to be known as Wester Hailes. As it took shape, Bridge No. 7 and the surrounding countryside, disappeared.

Wester Hailes represented stark reality for the country's first canal campaigning organisation, the Scottish Inland Waterways Association, set up in Edinburgh in 1971. A pipeline, over a mile long, had been installed to keep the water flowing while above ground the channel was filled in, landscaped and surrounded by houses, flats and roads. The prospect of getting such a complex blockage removed seemed vanishingly remote, but those early campaigners were not short of optimism, always hoping, while never quite envisaging something as transformative as the National Lottery. In preparing a bid for funding from the Millennium Commission, British Waterways realised that their main challenge was not technical, but personal and began to engage with the local community to demonstrate that a canal could be a positive asset for the area. Local opinion proved broadly supportive and, with funding in place, work began, but before the channel was cut, new bridges rose like islands out of a sea of muddy earth, as this picture from April 2001 shows.

Although the canal had been eliminated, its former route, pinched and compromised in places and crossed by a number of roads and paths could still be traced through the housing scheme. To reinstate it the engineers and contractors had to build seven new road bridges and two footbridges, including replacements for the bridge at Kingsknowe and Bridge No. 7. These were all made of reinforced concrete and embellished with the Union Canal name and the Roman numeral MM, signifying the second millennium. The reopening took place in August 2001. It rained, but that didn't dampen the spirits of those who had invested so much emotion and energy in making the impossible happen. A flotilla of boats of all shapes and sizes sailed along the remade channel, a sight that would have had the planners of the 1960s rubbing their eyes in disbelief. Leading the boats under the one bridge that didn't have to be rebuilt is a boat owned by British Waterways and given the name of the canal restoration scheme, *The Millennium Link*.

The Union Canal was a remarkable feat of engineering, a thirty-one mile long channel cut across undulating country at a height above sea level of 242 feet. It crossed great river valleys, was driven through cuttings, placed atop embankments and swung through right-angled bends, one of which is in the background of this picture of Calder Quay. Situated just to the west of Bridge No. 7 the canal at this point runs in a north/south direction. An empty rowing boat sits at the canal edge. It is typical of the kind of boats that hirers, based at Lochrin Basin or Slateford, offered for pleasure boating. It has a comfortable cradle-like seat for a passenger to relax while their companion propelled the craft with a couple of sweeps pivoted on thole-pins that the hirer could remove while the boat was waiting for a customer. It is speculation of course, but the person who hired this boat could have been the photographer, who has left it in the picture to add interest.

The canal resumes its east/west line after another sharp bend seen through the arch of Easter Hermiston Bridge, No. 9, which also frames a distant view of Arthur's Seat. The picture was taken in the 1950s, but if replicated some 30 years later the stretch of water just beyond the arch would look very different following construction of an aqueduct over the Edinburgh By-Pass Road by Lothian Regional Council's highways department. Canal campaigners were alarmed by the early proposals for this major road. These showed the canal being severed by a culvert and, with the Wester Hailes blockage just around the corner this would have made future restoration of the channel much harder. There was great relief when, after a hard-fought campaign the decision was taken to put the road in a cutting and carry the canal across it on a new aqueduct. Originally known as the Hermiston Aqueduct it has since been renamed the Scott Russell Aqueduct after a visionary naval architect, John Scott Russell.

John Scott Russell, whose name was given to the new aqueduct over the Edinburgh By-Pass Road, made an important observation when watching boat trials near Hermiston. He noticed that when a boat stopped suddenly the wave it was pushing in front of the bow kept going. He followed this wave for a couple of miles before it dissipated on bends in the canal and concluded that if a vessel could ride this bow wave it would have major implications for ship design. Sadly his visionary thinking was too advanced for the technologies of the day, although he later worked on other aspects of ship design with Isambard Kingdom Brunel and the perpetual wave, or soliton, generated as an electronic pulse, has been of value to the modern world. Hermiston, where this scientific discovery was made, was always a lovely spot, with the lawns in front of Hermiston House reaching down to the canal and the adjacent farm, seen here, the epitome of rural life on the edge of the city.

Ratho was that curious mix of a community engaged in an extractive industry set in farming country. Here the industry was quarrying, with large operations to the west of the village on both sides of the canal; one quarry has since been roofed and converted into a climbing centre. The men on the left of this picture look like industrial workers, but they were actually engaged in the ancient rural craft of blacksmithing, the cart wheels behind them a clear indication of a smithy. The picture looks north toward the canal bridge, with on the right, beside the lamp standard, a path that led down to the canal wharf where barges delivered coal to the adjacent gasworks. The blacksmiths probably got their furnace coal from there. Beyond the smithy, the last of the buildings running up to the bridge was a pub, the Bridge Inn, one of many in and around Ratho frequented by those noted drouths: canal boatmen, quarrymen and agricultural workers.

The canal had closed and the Bridge Inn was struggling when a new owner, Ronnie Rusack moved in. A scion of the famous Rusack's Hotel family in St Andrews, Ronnie was steeped in the catering trade and, allied to a love of boats the run-down village pub by the canal was the perfect outlet for his enthusiasms. He gave the Bridge Inn a makeover and established a reputation for quality dining. Then, in 1974, he took that onto the canal, launching a restaurant boat, the *Pride of the Union*. The canal was in a dreadful state. Closed for nearly a decade and neglected before that, there was barely enough water to float the boat, but after a Herculean effort by all concerned the channel was cleared. Freed from the silt, the boat proved such a success that a second restaurant boat the *Countess of Edinburgh*, later renamed *Pride of Belhaven* was also put on. By the time a day trip boat, *Ratho Princess*, had joined the fleet both the Bridge Inn and Ratho had been transformed.

The reinvention of both the inn and village was helped by events like the Pumpathon, a rally of vintage fire engines, seen in this picture from 1996 taken from the top of a turntable ladder (no drones in those days!). Two fire engines are in the lower left corner, while slipping under the bridge is the *St. John Crusader II*, a boat belonging to the Seagull Trust, a charitable body dedicated to providing canal cruises for disabled people. The Trust was set up by the Rev. Hugh Mackay, vice-chairman of the Scottish Inland Waterways Association whose fund-raising activities culminated in a trip boat, the *St. John Crusader*, being put on the canal at Ratho in 1979. The *Mackay Seagull*, named in honour of the charity's founder, joined in 1986 and the addition of a reception centre helped to enhance the cruising experience from Ratho. Another Seagull Trust boathouse was also established on the Union Canal at Falkirk.

To the west of Ratho the canal passes through a tranquil cutting that once resounded to the din of quarrying and then emerges into open country, where the modern din is provided by the M8 motorway. The road is alongside only briefly, brought close by a sweeping bend in the canal to the east of Clifton Hall Mains, where this picture of what looks like three men in a very small boat was taken in the 1950s. The canal was still open at this time and although dulled by wintry weather looks to be in reasonably good condition. Having just cleared Nellfield Bridge, No. 16, the men are heading west toward a secluded cutting adjacent to Clifton Hall. When the canal was being dug here, the tusk of a prehistoric woolly mammoth was unearthed. It was a find of significant antiquarian interest but, while the landowner and canal company debated its ownership, the navvies sold it to an Edinburgh toymaker. Horrified, the landowner dashed to the city to retrieve the tusk, or what remained of it, which he put on display in Clifton Hall.

The Almond Aqueduct, between Ratho and Broxburn is the shortest of the three great Union Canal aqueducts. It was built to the same pattern as the others, with the water contained in a stone-clad iron trough supported by hollow buttressed piers and five 50 feet span arches. Just to the east of the aqueduct is the entry point for the canal's principal water feeder, itself a remarkable piece of engineering. The water is extracted from the River Almond by a weir and sluice about three miles south of the canal. From there, a lade, like a mini canal runs beside the west bank of the river, crosses to the east bank on a superb little cast iron aqueduct and clings to the increasingly steep valley side as it takes the water down to the canal. When the Almond feeder was made, mill owners on the river were concerned about the possible loss of water, so the canal company made the huge Cobbinshaw Reservoir, in the hills to the south, to compensate for the extracted water and ensure that the river wouldn't run dry.

Following the canal's closure in 1965 it was blocked by a number of culverts, which were mainly built to replace existing bridges although a couple were installed to allow new roads to be built. One of these was the Dechmont to Newhouse section of the M8 motorway, which crossed the canal between the Almond Aqueduct and Broxburn. It was built between 1968 and 1970, and with the canal not long closed the decision to culvert the canal wasn't surprising. It wasn't clever either because the road didn't just block the channel it severed the towpath too, destroying it for people who wanted to use it as a cross-country walkway or cycle route. What made it worse was that, with a slightly different elevation the road could have cleared the canal, and when navigation was restored in the year 2000 sufficient headroom was gained by a relatively modest diversion of the channel that took it to a higher point on the road. The blocked and weed-choked canal is seen here looking east in 1994.

Broxburn was a small village on the main highway between Edinburgh and the west that became even better connected in 1822 with the completion of the canal, a new kind of highway. As part of the canal's facilities, a basin known as Port Buchan was created beside the main road, just to the east of the older and larger community of Uphall. The little canal port was thus well placed for passenger and goods traffic, but with Broxburn's later industry and the main railway line being developed to the east, the little port declined. It looked forlorn and deserted in the years following the canal's closure, but in early May 2000, Port Buchan had its day in the sun. The first section of the canal to be ceremonially reopened was that between Broxburn and Ratho. A flotilla of boats, seen here assembling at Port Buchan sailed east to the M8 where a celebration of the newly reinstated canal was held, before the boats carried on to Ratho. As more sections of canal were reopened there were more celebrations, but Port Buchan was where the renaissance began.

The canal may have brought some commercial activity to Broxburn, but the industry that turned the village into a town was shale oil. The pioneering genius behind it was James 'Paraffin' Young who began distilling oil from cannel coal at Bathgate in 1851 and, when supplies of that mineral dwindled, experimented with shale. He set up his huge Addiewell oil works in 1864, but prior to that, in 1861 a Robert Bell had started up a small oil works at Broxburn. A number of others were also set up in the area, but didn't amount to much until, in 1877, they were all drawn into one large concern, the Broxburn Oil Company. It became one of the industry's big players, with a large refinery on one side of the canal close to Greendykes Road and an oil works on the other. The canal's fortunes might have improved if this huge new industry had used it, but instead it was largely ignored except when water was needed to extinguish fires at the works. The Broxburn refinery and its adjacent Albyn works closed in 1927.

The scale of the oil industry is evident from the bings of spent shale that dominate the country between Broxburn and Winchburgh, where the large Niddry Castle oil works defied economic gravity longer than most, staying open until 1960. Oil was not Winchburgh's only industry because, situated beside the canal to the west of the village, was Alexander Dougal & Sons' brick and tile works. It worked the local blue clay and, although connected to the adjacent Edinburgh & Glasgow Railway line, much of the company's output was despatched by canal. They had their own horses, which could be changed at company stables when they got tired. The men were less fortunate, having to deliver their load and return, sleeping on the boat if they had to, and these were unsophisticated tubs with no creature comforts. The brickworks was the canal's last commercial operator, stopping sailings when the aqueduct over Slateford Road in Edinburgh was rebuilt in 1937. A remnant of the old works is on the right of this undated mid 20th century picture.

The boats in the foreground of this picture are typical of the barges used to transport heavy and bulky loads. They were known as scows, an old Scots word which is also used in America and has similarities to northern European words for barges or flat-bottomed boats. It is not clear from the picture whether the boat on the left was being loaded or unloaded and indeed what its cargo was. It clearly wasn't bricks, but could have been coal, stone, clinker or some other mineral, but whatever it was, it is a fascinating and unusual view of working boats on the canal around 1900. They are pulled in to a winding hole on the west side of Myre Bridge, No. 33, itself situated to the west of the Winchburgh brickworks. The men were evidently not expecting much traffic, having left one boat to float free and effectively block the channel. If the canal wasn't busy, neither was the towpath where the horse, with contented uninterest seemed happy to munch something tasty on the verge.

Craigton Bridge, No. 35, was more ornate than the standard pattern canal bridges and almost identical to Viewforth Bridge in Edinburgh. Instead of stone parapets it had decorative iron railings set between octagonal stone posts and the keystones were carved with Hopetoun family monograms. The road that crossed the bridge led to Hopetoun House. There was a small wharf beside the bridge, seen here in a derelict state in the 1950s. Its use, or uses, can only be guessed at. It could have served the estate, taking farm produce to market, or been an outlet for stone from the nearby Craigton Quarry. Incoming cargoes might have included coal, luggage or manure, a regular commodity carried on the canal from urban areas to enrich canalside fields. The canal here is in a largely rural setting, but just to the west was another huge shale-oil works.

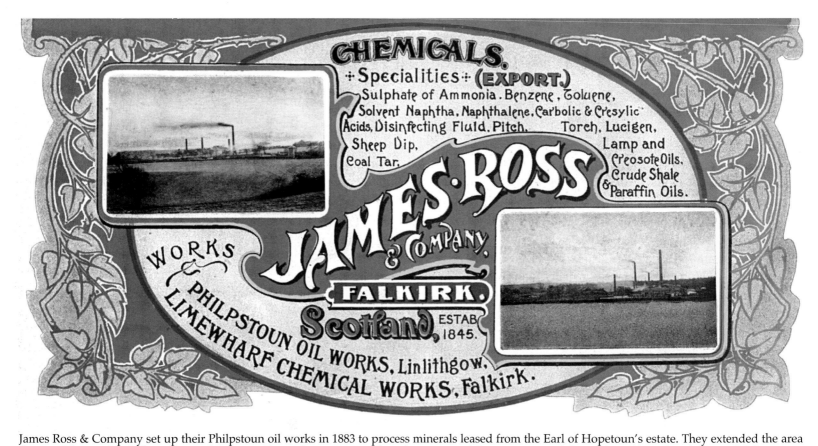

CHEMICALS.

Specialities (EXPORT.)

Sulphate of Ammonia. Benzene, Toluene, Solvent Naphtha. Naphthalene. Carbolic & Cresylic Acids, Disinfecting Fluid. Pitch. Torch, Lucigen, Sheep Dip, Coal Tar. Lamp and Creosote Oils. Crude Shale & Paraffin Oils.

JAMES·ROSS & COMPANY.

FALKIRK. Scotland, ESTAB 1845.

WORKS PHILPSTOUN OIL WORKS, Linlithgow. LIMEWHARF CHEMICAL WORKS, Falkirk.

James Ross & Company set up their Philpstoun oil works in 1883 to process minerals leased from the Earl of Hopetoun's estate. They extended the area they could mine for shale to the neighbouring Champfleurie Estate when they acquired the operations of the Bridgend-based Linlithgow Oil Company when it failed in 1902. With more shale to process, an expanded workforce and modern retorts the Philpstoun works made a variety of products, some of which were sent for further processing at the company's chemical works at Lime Wharf on the Forth & Clyde Canal at Falkirk. The product for which the works was perhaps best known was petrol, fuelling, literally the next great transport revolution, but ironically, the growth in car ownership mirrored the works' decline. It closed in 1931. By this time the operation had generated a huge amount of spent shale, which was piled on both sides of the canal in bings that had become so big and so steep they looked like the sides of a deep, forbidding canyon.

On its route between Edinburgh and Falkirk the canal passed a number of villages and came close to Uphall, but the most significant town on its route was Linlithgow. The main part of the town, with its lovely Scots vernacular buildings, imposing palace and St Michael's Church was on a lower level to the canal, which stuck to the high ground to the south. A little port, the Manse Road Basin, was created and used for coal, cargo handling and as a stopping place for the passenger boats. Horses could also be changed here at a little stables building. The basin must have been busy to begin with, but will have struggled following the opening in 1842 of the Edinburgh & Glasgow Railway, which squeezed between the town and the canal. After the canal's closure, an air of neglect hung over the basin but that was reversed when the Linlithgow Union Canal Society was formed in 1975. They brought the canal back to life and in 1978 introduced a delightful, diesel-powered replica Victorian steamboat, *Victoria* seen here in the centre of the picture surrounded by other boats.

No matter how busy Manse Road Basin was during the first twenty years, it's unlikely to have seen anything on the scale of activity generated by the Linlithgow Union Canal Society. They converted the former stables building into Scotland's only canal museum, opened a tearoom, and set up an activity centre. Boat rallies and festivals were held in the basin and the society also hosted daft events like cardboard boat races and the Drambuie Canal Marathon (see page 48). They also added other boats to their fleet, but in the early days there was a problem. Following closure, a drowned culvert was installed to carry Preston Road over the canal, blocking the navigation to the west of the basin. The society's boats could go east, but to the west were confined to a short stretch of water, a melancholy situation that prevailed until the 1990s, when the West Lothian Canal Project provided funding to replace the culvert with a bridge. The picture from c.1900 shows the canal looking west from Manse Road Basin.

The West Lothian Canal Project also restored navigation at a section of embankment to the west of Linlithgow that was breached in the 1980s. Throughout its history the Union Canal was prone to leaks and breaches, but this incident was serious. It occurred when the canal was closed, which meant there was no money to carry out an extensive repair and so dams were put in at each end of the breach to stop it getting worse, and prevent further flooding. The navigation was thus completely blocked, as was the towpath (although intrepid pedestrians ignored the signs), and this temporary arrangement was in place for so long that it got a name: the Kettlestoun Breach. The Kettlestoun name has a more positive place in canal history as the location of a quarry that produced many boatloads of stone. Both it and the breached embankment were to the east of Kettlestoun Bridge, No. 47, seen here about 1910. The parapet railings have since been replaced with brick walls and tell tale rubble in the undergrowth beside the towpath is all that remains of the cottage on the left.

With the Kettlestoun Breach repaired and Preston Road cleared, the Linlithgow Union Canal Society could sail their boats from Manse Road Basin to the most spectacular feature on the canal, the Avon Aqueduct. Built to the same specification as the Slateford and Almond Aqueducts, it is special because at 810 feet and incorporating twelve arches it is the second longest aqueduct in Britain. And because it is difficult to get to by road, the best way to see it is to go by canal, which adds to its appeal for canal enthusiasts. The picture, taken in the 1950s, looks east from a point close to the Causewayend Basin, a trans-shipment basin associated with an attempt in 1840 to create an inter-city rail/canal passenger link before the Edinburgh and Glasgow Railway was built. It was based on a series of early railways that ran through the Monklands and across the Slamannan Plateau. These lines were connected to the basin so that passenger boats could link up with trains, but the boats struggled to stick to scheduled timings and the scheme failed.

In a guidebook for canal boat passengers, published in 1823, Polmont House and its situation were described as 'extremely rural and retired'. That changed with the arrival of the railway and a new station, which encouraged significant housing development, a trend that has continued into modern times. This early 20th century picture looking east from the approach to Brightons Bridge, No. 54, shows housing and steadings at Whitesideloan in a view that has since been transformed by modern housing and tree growth. While the railway influenced urban growth, the canal's impact was felt mainly on the moorland to the south where coal owners like the Duke of Hamilton opened mines to supply the newly available Edinburgh market. The coal was carted to the canal and loaded onto barges at a basin and wharf just west of the bridge. The wharf was also convenient for the nearby quarry and as a maintenance depot.

Referring to Redding, the 1823 guidebook for canal boat passengers described 'the trees that shade this village', while also noting that the Duke of Hamilton had opened his new Reddanrig Colliery 'close upon the south bank of the canal'. The coal industry subsequently had a major influence on the village, but it was a colliery on the north bank that became front-page news in 1923. Men in Redding No. 23 pit were working up to a barrier known as the Universal Dyke when accumulated water in the older Nos. 4 and 5 pits, burst in on them. Forty men died in this, the worst flooding disaster in a Scottish colliery. Also at Redding, opposite the colliery on the south bank of the canal, was Nobel's chemical works where explosives used in the mining and other extractive industries were made. Its significance locally is clear from this postcard, which was captioned 'canal near Nobel's factory' although it shows, Purliehill Easter Bridge, No. 57, which was situated about 1,000 yards to the west.

One of the major difficulties encountered when planning the Union Canal was not so much the terrain as who owned it. The route crossed many large estates whose owners drove a hard bargain, but one who proved especially obdurate was William Forbes of Callendar House. He reacted badly to the idea of coal barges passing along a canal close to the big house and forced the engineers to take a more southerly route and cut a tunnel through Prospect Hill. The great man died before work began, but try as they might the canal owners couldn't change the minds of the estate trustees and the tunnel had to be excavated for 690 yards through solid rock. The Irish navvies – local men found the work too hard – cut the rock up to a height where it would stand without support, and wide enough for a towpath. The portals were faced with dressed stone. The two men in the picture are standing with their dog in the deep cutting at the west end of the tunnel.

When first built the canal ran for three-quarters of a mile between the tunnel and the top of the lock flight that linked it to the Forth & Clyde Canal. It is a splendid section of canal, although perhaps best appreciated from the towpath, which affords wonderful views across Falkirk to the Ochil Hills and the higher mountains of the north. The views can of course be seen from the water, something that the Seagull Trust recognised when they built a boathouse at Bantaskine as a base for their *Govan Seagull*, a boat built by shipyard apprentices in Glasgow and launched in 1984. Earlier generations of boaters also enjoyed messing about on this stretch of water, in the small rowing boats seen here lined up beside a so-called 'boating station' situated at the top of the locks. People could please themselves where they rowed, sometimes venturing up to and even through the tunnel. Lying alongside, beyond the rowing boats, is a maintenance barge.

The flight of locks at the western end of the Union Canal swept down the hillside in a curving line that ended in a wide basin known as Port Downie, named after Robert Downie of Appin, the chairman of the company. The basin was connected to the Forth & Clyde Canal just above its Lock 16. There were eleven locks in the flight, each one 69 feet long, twelve feet six inches wide and with a drop of ten feet – a total fall of 110 feet. Such a large lock flight took a long time to negotiate, so the fast daytime passenger boats didn't use it and stayed on their respective canals while their customers changed boats by walking up or down beside the locks. The delays caused by the locks proved to be their downfall and, in 1933, with boat movements reduced to virtually nil the flight was closed and dismantled, severing the connection between the canals. The picture, which dates from 1906 shows the locks covered in snow. The level line on the high ground behind the locks indicates an extension to the canal, which was made to reduce the distance boat passengers had to walk.

The extended section of canal above the locks ended bluntly at a terminal basin known as Port Maxwell. It is seen here in 1978 with competitors preparing to take part in the Drambuie Marathon, one of the more idiosyncratic boating activities that took place after the closure of the canal. The object was for crews of two to drive, paddle or manhandle their inflatable boats and outboard engines from Glasgow to Edinburgh, and to do it at a set speed, which was not easy when portaging round obstructions or contending with the ever-present hazards of weed and rubbish. Some large obstacles like the M8 blockage or the Wester Hailes infill were bypassed using a motor vehicle driven by a back-up crew, but smaller obstructions had to be negotiated by the crews themselves. It was a peculiar form of masochism that became an eagerly anticipated feature of the canal calendar from the late 1970s to the early 1990s and for much of that time it was expertly organised by the Linlithgow Union Canal Society.